Adapted and published in the United States
in 1986 by Silver Burdett Company,
Morristown, New Jersey

Library of Congress Cataloging-in-Publication Data

Kerrod, Robin.
    Structures and materials.

    (Understanding)
    Includes index.
    Summary: Describes some of the world's natural
materials, such as minerals, and man-made, such as
plastics, and the esthetic and functional uses to
which they have been put, particularly in the
construction of buildings and bridges.
    1. Materials—Juvenile literature.   2. Structural
engineering—Juvenile literature.   [1. Materials.
2. Structural engineering]   I. Phillpotts, Beatrice.
II. Title.   III. Series.
TA403.2.K47   1986   620.1'1   85-27782
ISBN 0-382-09182-5

Designer
Julian Holland

Picture researcher
Stella Martin

Artists
Fred Anderson
Hayward & Martin Ltd
Sarah Pooley

Editor
Beatrice Phillpotts

Adviser
Sue Becklake

Photo Credits:
Airship Industries (UK) Ltd
Ajax News & Feature Service
All-Sport Photographic Ltd
Biofotos
British Aerospace
British Petroleum Company plc
British Steel Corporation
J Allan Cash Ltd
Ciba-Geigy Plastics
Bruce Coleman Ltd
Computervision Ltd
De Beers
Susan Griggs Agency Ltd
Robert Harding Picture Library
Michael Holford
Alan Hutchinson Library
Institute of Geological Sciences
Robin Kerrod
Lawrence Radiation Laboratory, California
S Martin
Mercedes-Benz (UK) Ltd
NASA
Natural History Photographic Agency
Palitoy
Spectrum Colour Library
ZEFA

Understanding
Structures
and
Materials

Robin Kerrod

Silver Burdett Company

Morristown, New Jersey

Contents

◁ Building a flour mill in Qatar.

Materials in the home

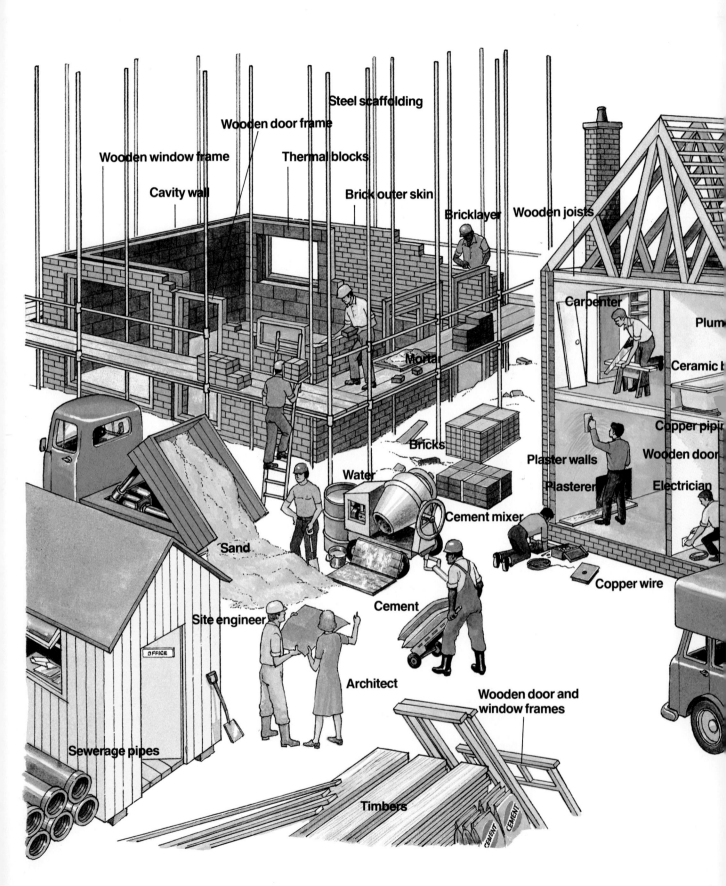

Steel scaffolding

Wooden door frame

Wooden window frame

Thermal blocks

Cavity wall

Brick outer skin

Bricklayer

Wooden joists

Carpenter

Plum

Ceramic t

Copper pipi

Wooden door

Plaster walls

Electrician

Plasterer

Mortar

Bricks

Water

Cement mixer

Copper wire

Sand

Cement

Site engineer

OFFICE

Architect

Wooden door and
window frames

Sewerage pipes

Timbers

CEMENT

Isn't it fascinating watching people at work on a building site? There is something interesting going on right from the very beginning. Trucks are continually coming and going, carrying cement, bricks, sand, timber, door and window frames, pipes, tiles, scaffolding and many more things besides. Teams of workers move in one after the other, playing their different parts as the houses rise gradually from the ground. You can gain an idea of the hustle and bustle of the building site from the picture.

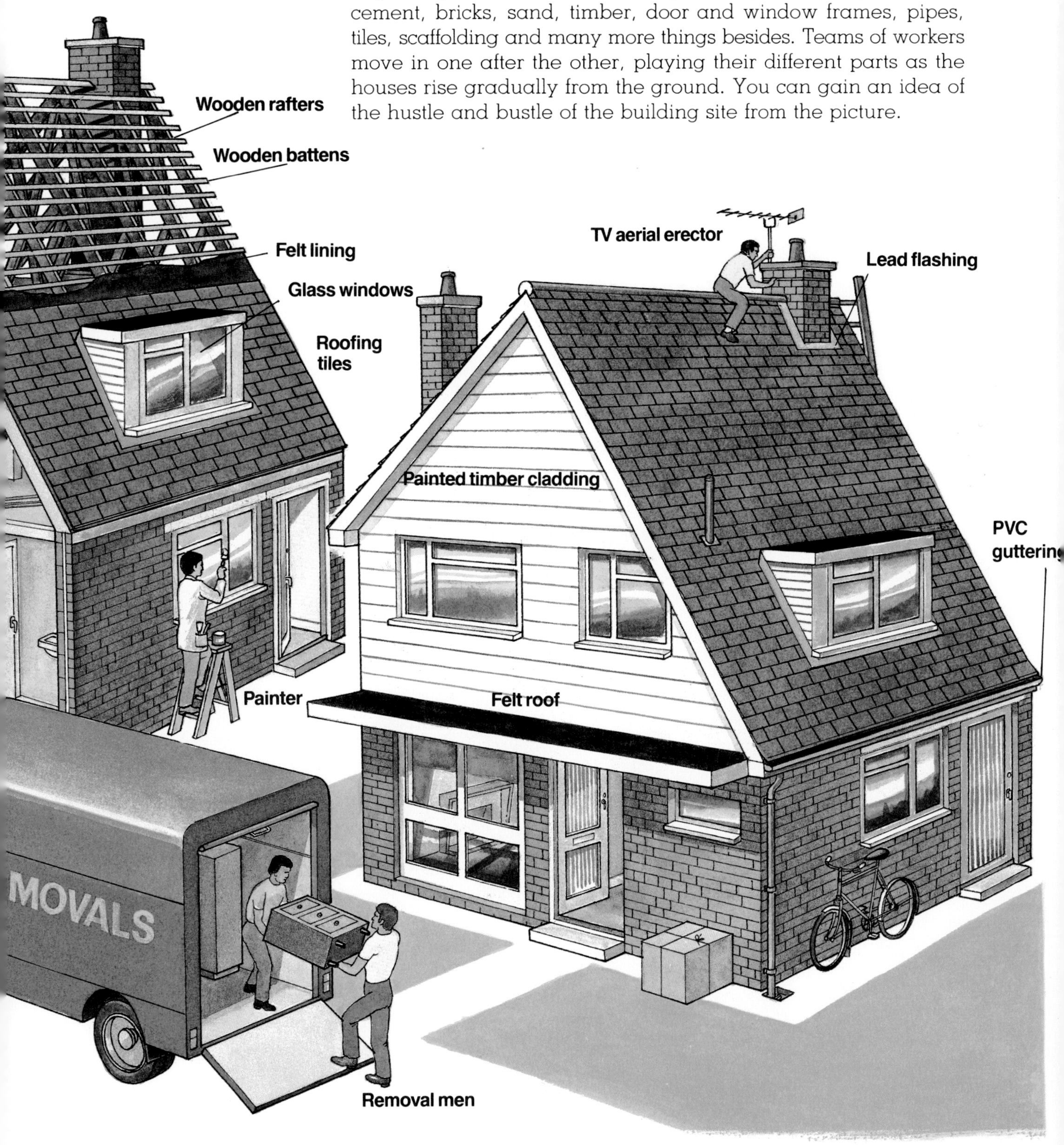

Wooden rafters

Wooden battens

Felt lining

Glass windows

Roofing tiles

TV aerial erector

Lead flashing

Painted timber cladding

PVC guttering

Painter

Felt roof

MOVALS

Removal men

If you kept a note of the amounts of materials that went into each house, you would be surprised—many tons of sand and cement, thousands of bricks, several trees (for the timber), hundreds of feet of copper tubing and wiring, and so on. Also, you mustn't forget the thousands of gallons of water used for making the concrete, mortar and plaster. Because of all this water, houses need quite a time to dry out before they can be decorated.

Cement and concrete

The first stage of housebuilding is laying the foundation. The foundation is what supports the house walls. It is always made of concrete. The concrete is poured into trenches dug into the ground by mechanical diggers. Often, the concrete arrives at the building site ready mixed in a mixer-truck. This has a rotating body to prevent the concrete inside from setting.

Concrete itself is made from a mixture of cement, sand, stone chips and water. Cement is a fine gray powder made by rotating chalk and other earthy materials in a rotating kiln. When the water is mixed with cement and it dries, a chemical reaction takes place, which changes it into a solid material as hard as rock.

Bricklaying

When the concrete foundation has dried, bricklaying can begin. Bricks are made by baking, or "firing" blocks of moist clay in kilns. Various colors of bricks can be obtained by including colored earth with the clay. The bricks are laid upon one another with a layer of mortar in between. Mortar is made from cement and sand, together with a little lime or with chemicals called plasticizers. The lime or plasticizers make the cement mixture easier to work. To give the walls strength, the bricks are laid so that the joints in the neighboring layers, or courses, are staggered.

The bricks form only part of the house walls. Inside the brick "shell" is another wall, built up of lightweight blocks, made from ash or something similar. Between the two walls is a cavity of about two inches. This cavity helps insulate the house against heat loss.

The cavity wall also prevents dampness from coming through from the outside. Dampness must also be prevented from coming up from the ground. That is why the walls are laid with a damp-proof course. This is simply a thin layer of bitumen or plastic. It is usually laid about six inches up from the ground.

Solids, liquids and gases

If you put a tray of water into the refrigerator, it will freeze, or change into hard ice. If you heat up water in a kettle, it will change into steam. Ice, water and steam are different forms of the same substance. We say they are different states. Ice is a solid, water is a liquid and steam is a gas.

All other substances, or different kinds of matter, exist on Earth either as a solid, a liquid or a gas. We call these the three states of matter. Like water, many other substances can also change their state if the temperature changes enough.

Take a rock, for example. We cannot think of anything more permanent. But if you heat it up to several thousand degrees, it will melt into a red-hot liquid. The red-hot lava that pours from volcanoes is a liquid rock.

We give different names to the various changes of states that substances undergo. When a solid changes into a liquid we say, it melts. When a liquid changes into a solid, we say it freezes. When a liquid changes into a gas, we say it vaporizes, or boils. And when a gas changes into a liquid, we say it condenses.

Solids

Most of the substances that exist on Earth are solids at normal temperatures — rocks, minerals, metals, wood, and so on. In general solids are hard and rigid. They have a definite shape, and it is usually difficult to change it.

Under suitable conditions, most pure substances in the solid state can form into a regular shape we call a crystal. And each substance always forms the same kind of crystal.

◁ This great cliff of granite is found in the Yosemite National Park in California. It is known as El Capitan. Granite is one of the hardest of the rocks, which resists the action of the weather. El Capitan was once buried under softer rock. It has remained nearly untouched, while the softer rock has long since been worn away by the action of rain, snow and ice. A piece of rock is a good example of a solid.

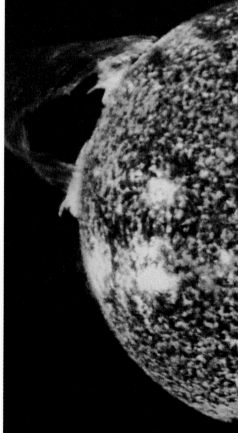

◁ *Snow is made up of billions of tiny ice crystals. They are formed when specks of water in the air freeze, or change from liquid into solid. This picture shows some snow crystals magnified many times. Nearly all of them are six-pointed, yet no two crystals are exactly alike.*

▽ *This picture of the Sun was taken by astronauts on the Skylab space station in 1973. The Sun is a huge ball of very hot gas. Inside the Sun the temperature rises to millions of degrees. At such temperatures the gases turn into a fourth state of matter, which we call plasma.*

Liquids

Liquids have quite different properties from solids. They have no definite shape. They simply take the shape of whatever container they are in. They are more affected by temperature than solids are. When we heat them, they expand quite a lot. We use this property in ordinary thermometers. They work because a column of silvery mercury or colored alcohol gets longer as the temperature rises, or gets shorter as the temperature drops.

When you push against a liquid, it moves, or flows — it is a

◁ This is a modern airship called the Skyship 600. It stays up in the sky because it contains a gas that is lighter than air. This gas is helium. It is the second lightest of all gases, after hydrogen.

◁ A pond skater "walking" on the surface of a pond. It can "walk" on water because all liquids have a kind of "skin." This skin is caused by a force known as surface tension.

fluid. The pressure you apply to a liquid is carried throughout the liquid. This principle is used in various hydraulic machines and devices, including the brakes on an automobile. When the driver wants to apply the brakes, pressure is applied to the foot pedal. This forces a piston against a liquid in pipes leading to the brakes. The liquid carries the foot pressure along the pipes, and this forces the brakes against the wheels.

Only one common substance exists in liquid form on Earth—water. It is estimated that there are about 1.5 million million million tons of water in the rivers, lakes and the oceans. Without this water, life as we know it could not exist.

Gases

Gases are different from solids and liquids because they have no size or shape. They will fill the whole of the vessel that contains them. When you apply pressure to a gas, it will flow. Like a liquid, it is a fluid. Also when you apply pressure, you compress the gas, or force it into a smaller space. We often find compressed gas very useful. We use it, for example, to provide air supplies for skin-divers swimming underwater.

The most common gas on Earth is the air all around us. It is actually a mixture of several gases. The main gases are nitrogen (which makes up about four-fifths of the air by volume) and oxygen (about one-fifth). It is the oxygen that we must breathe to live.

Atoms and elements

Our world is made up of millions of different things — rocks, plants, animals, air, water, bicycles, matchboxes, paper, the Earth, the Sun, the planets. This list is endless. These things are all different forms of matter.

What is matter made of? If you could take all these things apart, you would find that they are made up from about 90 different basic building blocks. We call them the chemical elements. Most of the substances we are familiar with are made up of two or more elements combined together. We call them chemical compounds. Wood, for example, is a compound containing the elements carbon, hydrogen and oxygen, combined together.

What are the elements made of? If you could cut up a piece of an element, say gold, smaller and smaller and smaller, you would eventually come to the smallest part that can exist. It is the atom, which is so tiny that ten million in a row would measure only a millimeter. If you could cut up all the elements in this way, you would find that they all had a slightly different kind of atom. What are the atoms like? If you could look inside one, you would find that it is mainly of tiny particles called protons and neutrons. This part is called the nucleus. Circling in a cloud around the nucleus are a number of even smaller particles, called electrons. There are always the same number of electrons as there are protons.

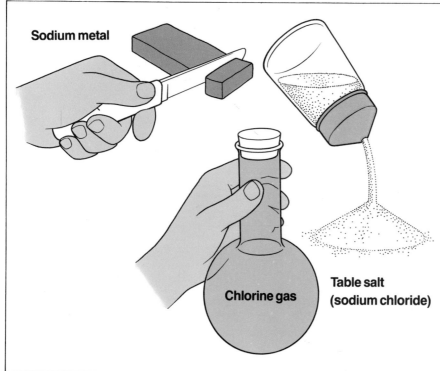

Sodium metal

Chlorine gas

Table salt (sodium chloride)

Most everyday substances are chemical compounds. They are made up of two or more of the chemical elements combined together. One common chemical compound we meet everyday is table salt. It is made up of the elements sodium and chlorine. Salt is harmless, but both sodium and chlorine are deadly. Sodium is a soft metal that can burn you. Chlorine is a colored poisonous gas that can kill you if you breathe enough of it.

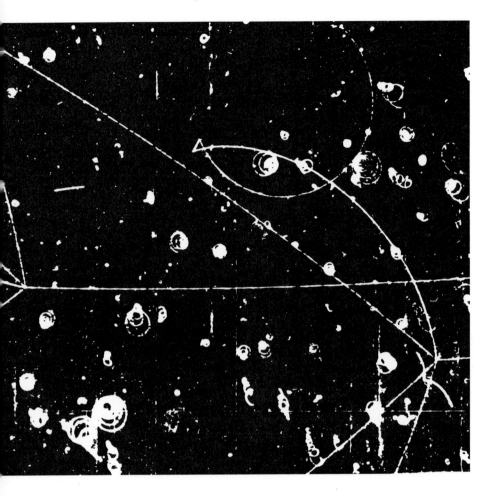

△This picture shows some tracks made by subatomic particles. The tracks are actually a line of tiny bubbles formed when the particles pass through a special chamber, called a bubble chamber. In several places in the picture you can see where a single track suddenly branches out into several tracks. This shows where one subatomic particle has knocked other particles out of an atom. When collision between particles takes place, we say that an "event" has occurred.

▷This is a model of the smallest unit, or molecule of a substance that is found in the cells of living things. It is known as DNA. DNA is a very special molecule that tells the living cells how to grow. It is made up of hundreds of atoms joined together, mainly carbon and hydrogen. The atoms form a long chain with a kind of spiral shape, called a double helix. The chain is made up of a string of carbon atoms, to which the other atoms are linked. Most molecules in living things are built up of a string of carbon atoms. Plastics also contain long chains of carbon atoms.

◁ *A nuclear power station near Schweinfurth in West Germany. For "fuel" it uses the element uranium. Uranium is unusual because its atoms can be made to split. When this happens, great heat is given out. In the power station the heat is used to boil water into steam. This is then used to drive the generators that make electricity.*

▽ *The different chemical elements are made up of different kinds of atoms. These atoms contain different numbers of protons, neutrons and electrons.*

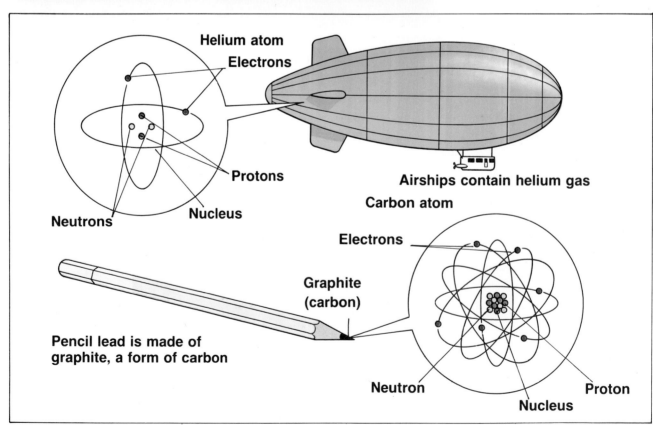

Helium atom

Electrons

Protons

Nucleus

Neutrons

Airships contain helium gas

Carbon atom

Electrons

Graphite (carbon)

Pencil lead is made of graphite, a form of carbon

Neutron

Nucleus

Proton

Rocks and minerals

The Earth is a great ball of rock hurtling through space. The Earth's crust, the surface we walk on, is made up of solid rock covered mostly with crumbly soil, sand, and mud. But far beneath the hard crust the rock is in a semi-liquid, or "plastic" state. It is also hot and under great pressure. We call this hot rock magma.

In some places, the Earth's crust is weak, and from time to time the magma underneath forces its way upward into cracks and cavities in the upper crust. In these cavities the magma cools slowly. Gradually the chemical substances it contains start coming out of the liquid in the form of mineral crystals. Eventually the whole rock becomes a solid mass of crystals, which may grow quite big. Granite is an example of a rock formed in this way. It is one kind of igneous rock.

Sometimes the liquid magma pushes right to the surface and shoots out into the air. This is what happens when a volcano erupts. The hot magma flows away from the volcano and cools quickly. It hardens into a rock we call lava, which is another igneous rock. Basalt is a common kind of dark lava.

▽*One of the magnificent underground caverns at Carlsbad in New Mexico. The Carlsbad Caverns were formed by water tunneling through the limestone rock. They are full of beautiful columns called stalagmites and stalactites. Stalagmites rise from the floor, and stalactites hang from the roof of the caverns. They are formed when water containing lime drips from the roof onto the floor. Some water evaporates and leaves behind tiny specks of limestone. These gradually build up into columns.*

◁ In the clear waters of the Red Sea, divers inspect a beautiful coral reef. Coral is a rock rather like limestone, but it was formed in a different way. It was made by living things — tiny creatures called corals. Corals grow on the seabed in warm waters. When they die, they leave behind their chalky skeletons, which build up to form the reefs. Eventually the reefs grow up to the surface, trap drifting seeds and debris, and in time form into islands. The many islands in the Pacific Ocean formed in this way.

▷ A piece of granite, one of the most attractive of our rocks. It is an igneous rock formed when magma cooled slowly inside the Earth's crust, allowing crystals to form. You can see the crystals in this lump of granite quite clearly. They are mainly pink, white and black. The pink crystals are of the mineral feldspar. The white ones are quartz, and the black ones are mica. Most rocks are made up of a mixture of minerals.

Sedimentary rocks

The rocks on the surface of the Earth look solid enough, but in time they start to crumble, under the action of the weather — rain, wind, snow and ice. The bits of broken rock are then often swept away by rivers. As they tumble over one another, the chips get smoothed into pebbles, then smaller and smaller particles. The action of the sea against shore rocks does the same thing. This wearing away of the rocks is known as erosion.

Erosion produces fine rocky materials such as gravel, sand, mud and clay. Over millions of years, layers of these materials may build up. Under very great pressure, the layers underneath change into hard rock. It is called sedimentary rock. Sandstone is a sedimentary rock formed from sand. Other sedimentary rocks formed when chemicals, such as calcium carbonate, were left behind when ancient seas dried up. Limestone is the rock formed in this way from calcium carbonate.

Metamorphic rocks

Existing rocks may also get changed in another way. They may come into contact with hot magma deep underground and start to melt. When they cool again, they have changed and often contain different minerals. Such changed rocks are called metamorphic rocks. They include marble and slate.

▷ *A stream of red-hot liquid rock pours from the Kilauea volcano in 1983. Kilauea, in Hawaii, is one of the most active volcanoes in the world. It erupts nearly every year. It is located at a point where the Earth's crust is weak. This allows molten rock from deep underground to force its way up to the surface. As the rock pours out, it soon cools and forms a grayish-black rock called lava. This often looks like cinders. Like most rocks lava is made up of a number of minerals mixed together. But you cannot see them as crystals. The rock cooled too quickly for crystals to form.*

Crystals

If you look at a piece of granite or a similar kind of rock, you will notice that it is made up of masses of shiny crystals, rather like bits of colored glass. They are crystals of the different minerals that make up the rock. As you can see, the crystals are of all shapes and sizes and are lumped haphazardly together.

In some rocks, however, you can sometimes find cracks or cavities containing perhaps only one kind of mineral. If there is plenty of room, the mineral will have formed into quite large crystals. And they will have a very distinctive shape. When you find other crystals of the same mineral, you will notice that they also have the same shape. When you find well-formed crystals of other minerals, you will probably notice that they have a different shape.

Two common shapes of mineral crystals are shown in the photographs on this page. Fluorite crystals have the shape of a cube. So have the crystals of rock salt and galena. Calcite crystals have a more complicated shape. They form clusters of long six-sided "fingers" tipped with pyramids.

▽ *These are crystals of the mineral fluorite. They have a cubic shape. Fluorite crystals may also be found in other colors, particularly blue. Many glow, or fluoresce when ultraviolet light shines on them.*

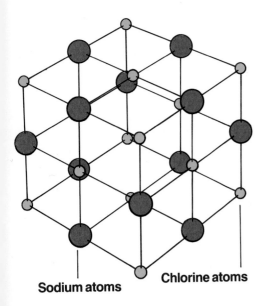

Sodium atoms   **Chlorine atoms**

△ *The space lattice of crystals of ordinary table salt, which is the chemical compound sodium chloride. In the lattice the atoms of sodium and chlorine are arranged alternately in the shape of a cube. Many other minerals have a cubic lattice. And, like salt, the minerals form crystals in the shape of a cube.*

The space lattice

If you accidentally drop a crystal, you often find that it breaks cleanly to give new flat faces. If you experiment further, you will find that crystals usually break, or cleave, in certain directions, or along certain planes. And the angles between the faces are always the same. In other words a crystal tends to keep its same basic shape no matter what size it is.

You can imagine that if you continued breaking the crystal again and again, you would eventually come to a basic unit of the same shape. We call this unit the space lattice. It is the framework in which the atoms of the crystal are arranged.

The atoms of the different elements in a crystal are arranged in a definite pattern within the lattice. In the salt (sodium chloride) lattice, for example, the sodium and chlorine atoms are arranged alternately. The whole framework forms the shape of a cube, and is called a cubic lattice. Altogether there are seven basic lattices which give rise to seven basic crystal shapes.

Gems and gemstones

Most kinds of crystals are attractive to look at in one way or another. Some of the most beautiful crystals are used in jewelry. Various kinds of colored quartz crystals are often used, including

△ *Beautiful crystals of the mineral calcite. For obvious reasons this form of the mineral is often called "dog-tooth" calcite. Calcite is one crystal form of calcium carbonate, one of the most common minerals in the Earth's crust. It is also sometimes found in a perfectly transparent form known as Iceland Spar.*

the violet amethyst and the smoky brown citrine. We call amethyst and citrine semi-precious stones, or gemstones. Other attractive gemstones include the red garnet, green beryl, red spinel and variously colored topaz and zircon.

All these gemstones are attractive, but are no match for the "Big Four" gems, diamond, emerald, sapphire and ruby. These gems flash and sparkle with unrivaled brilliance and are very hard and therefore cannot be so easily damaged. They are also very rare, which makes them very expensive. Emeralds are rare forms of the mineral beryl. They have a glorious green color. Rubies and sapphires are rare varieties of a common mineral called corundum. Rubies are fiery red in color, sapphires are a glorious blue.

Diamonds are usually a clear white in color, but may sometimes be colored. Blue diamonds are the rarest. Diamonds are found deep underground in rock formations called pipes, or in the sand and gravel of riverbeds. The main diamond mines are in South Africa.

Many of the diamonds mined are not good enough for gems. But they are useful in industry for cutting and polishing operations because they are so hard.

△These diamonds are worth a fortune. Diamonds are the most prized of all gems. They are all rare, and have a unique sparkle and brilliance because of the way they reflect and refract (bend) light. But the shapes you see here are not natural. When they were mined, these diamonds looked like dull pieces of glass. Their true beauty has been revealed by expert cutting, which gave them their many little faces, or facets, to catch the light to best advantage.

Experiment!

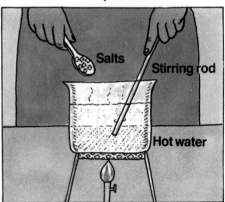

Pour some salts (such as Epsom salts) into a beaker of hot water, and stir until no more dissolve. Then take the beaker off the heat and allow the solution to cool.

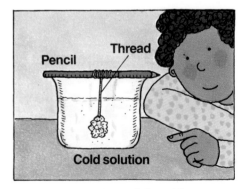

Next, dangle a piece of thread into the cold solution. You will find that crystals will start to grow around it.

Mineral fuels

The most important fuels the world uses today are coal, oil and natural gas. We get them from the ground by various forms of mining, and we often call them the "mineral" fuels. But they are not like ordinary minerals, which are inorganic (non-living) materials. The mineral fuels are organic materials — they are the remains of things that once lived. Coal is the remains of huge plants. Oil and natural gas are the remains of minute organisms that lived in ancient seas.

People have been mining coal for hundreds of years, and there should be enough coal to last us for several centuries to come. People began extracting oil in the mid-1800s, but only in the last 50 years has it been used in vast quantities. About 1500 million gallons of oil are now used every day throughout the world. At this rate it is expected that the world will run out of oil early in the next century.

Extracting coal

Some coal lies close to the surface and can often be simply dug out, using power shovels and excavators. This is called opencast mining. But much coal lies deep underground. The coal seams are reached by sinking shafts vertically into the ground, and then driving tunnels horizontally from the shafts.

▷ *An opencast coal mine at Frechen in West Germany. Opencast mining can take place when the coal deposit lies on or close to the surface. The method is simple. Any soil lying on top of the coal seams is removed. Then the coal is broken up and loaded into trucks or railroad cars for removal. In practice this is not as easy as it sounds. Usually vast quantities of soil have to be removed to reach the seam. This is necessary at the mine shown in the picture. Mammouth excavators are working at different levels to strip away the soil, until the coal (bottom) is exposed.*

Drilling for Oil

Oil (which is properly called petroleum) is extracted from the ground through boreholes drilled deep into the rocks. Oil gets trapped in certain rock formations, such as an arch of solid rock, and forms a pool, or reservoir there.

Where oil engineers think there is a likely oil trap, they set up a drilling rig and bore a hole down to it. They use a method called rotary drilling — drilling with a rotating toothed bit on the end of a long "string" of drill pipes. They now drill at sea as well as on land. Some of the biggest oil finds in recent years have been made offshore, for example, in the North Sea.

If the oil engineers do strike oil, they line the borehole with steel pipes, fit valves on top, and pipe the oil into the storage tanks. The oil is eventually transported by pipeline or tanker to the oil refineries. Here it is treated in various ways to make it into useful products. It is first separated into various parts, or "fractions," which are liquids such as gasoline and kerosene.

▽ *The black "mineral" we know as coal is the remains of giant plants that grew hundreds of millions of years ago. It is a kind of fossil. Today layers, or seams of coal can be found near the surface or deep underground. Coal mining is one of the world's great industries.*

350 million years ago giant trees and ferns grew in the tropical swamps that covered the Earth.

The trees died, fell into the swamps and started to decay. Thick layers of decaying matter built up.

Over millions of years the layers became pressed down by layers of earth and formed hard seams.

▷*This pump is pumping oil to the surface from an underground well in Bahrain. It is nicknamed a "nodding donkey." Bahrain is one of the many places in the Persian Gulf where there are vast deposits of oil. When the oil comes to the surface, it is sent by pipeline to the nearest port. Then tankers take it to oil refineries in other countries.*

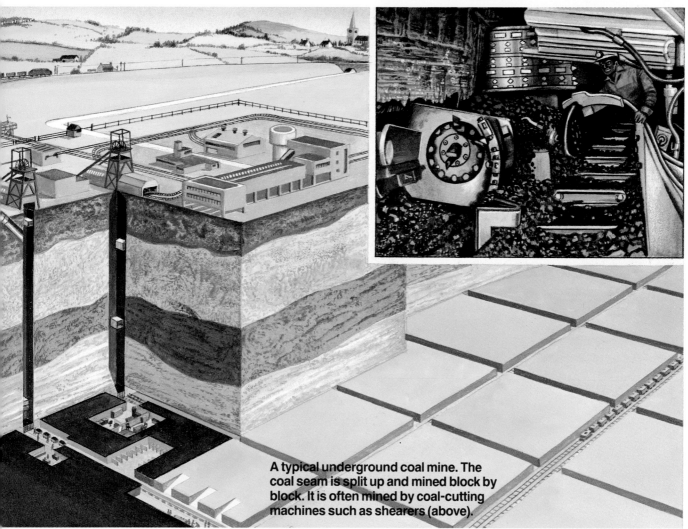

A typical underground coal mine. The coal seam is split up and mined block by block. It is often mined by coal-cutting machines such as shearers (above).

Metals

Of all the hundreds of different materials we use everyday, the most important by far are the metals. Without the strength of steel, we could not build bridges and skyscrapers. Without the electrical properties of copper, we wouldn't have electricity. In general without metals we would still be in the Stone Age.

Out of the 90 or so chemical elements found in nature, about 70 are classed as metals, but only about a quarter of them are very important. The most important metal of all is iron, because it can be made into steel, our main constructional material. Aluminum, copper, tin, lead, nickel, chromium, manganese, magnesium, zinc, gold, silver, and platinum are also of vital importance.

Extracting metals

Gold, silver and platinum are different from the other metals listed above because they are found in metal form in the ground. The other metals are not. We get these other metals by processing certain minerals, which contain the metal element combined with other chemical elements. These minerals are called ores.

▽ *This Nazca mask came from Iquitos, in Peru. It was made by native craftsmen nearly 2000 years ago. Yet it still has a beautiful color and shine. This is because it is made of gold. Gold does not corrode, or "rust" away like many other metals. Gold was one of the first metals used because it could be found "native," or in metal form, in the ground. It is still highly prized for its beauty.*

We usually extract a metal from its ores by a heating process, called smelting. Iron, for example, is made by smelting iron ore with coke and limestone in a blast furnace. This is so called because hot air is blasted through it to make it burn fiercely.

Aluminum is extracted from its ore, bauxite, in a rather different way. The aluminum mineral in bauxite is first separated out by means of chemical solutions. It is next mixed with another aluminum mineral and melted in a furnace. Then electricity is passed through the molten mass, and breaks down the aluminum minerals into aluminum metal. This kind of process is called electrolysis.

Some metals can be dissolved out of their ores by acid or another chemical. Some copper is obtained in this way. Its ore is treated with acid, and a copper solution forms. Copper metal is then obtained by passing electricity through the solution.

▽Copper forms the connecting links, or circuits, on this printed-circuit board. Boards like this are used in computers and other electronic equipment. Copper is widely used in all kinds of electrical work because it passes electric current easily. We say it is a good conductor of electricity. It is also a good conductor of heat. Copper is sometimes used for ornaments because it has an attractive reddish-brown color.

▷ Molten iron running from a blast furnace. Iron is made by heating iron ore with coke and limestone in a blast furnace. The coke acts as fuel for the furnace and also changes the iron ore into iron metal. The limestone helps form an earthy slag, which removes unwanted impurities from the iron. The iron from the blast furnace is often called pig iron because it is sometimes run into molds called pigs. Pig iron is not pure enough to be used by itself. It has to be refined, or purified.

◁ Like most aircraft, this plane is made mainly of aluminum. Aluminum is a strong metal, like iron. But it has one great advantage over iron — it is much lighter. It is therefore ideal as a material for building aircraft, which must be as light as possible. It has another advantage over iron — it does not corrode, or "rust." Aluminum also has many uses in the home. It is used for pots and pans, kitchen foil and bottle tops, window frames and greenhouses.

Alloys

The most important metal we use today is steel. But it is not a pure metal. It is made up mainly of iron, but it also contains small quantities of other metals, such as manganese, and it also contains small quantities of carbon. We call such a metal mixture an alloy. Most of the metals we use today are alloys.

Many coppery-colored coins are made of bronze, an alloy of copper and tin. Many silvery-colored coins are made of cupronickel, an alloy of copper and nickel. Our ordinary cutlery is made of stainless steel, an alloy of iron, chromium and nickel.

▽*An Etruscan artist made this bronze statuette in about 500 B.C. The Etruscans lived in northern Italy. Bronze was the first metal that was used on a large scale. This happened in the so-called Bronze Age period of history. Bronze is an alloy of copper and tin. It is useful for making statues because it can be shaped easily by casting.*

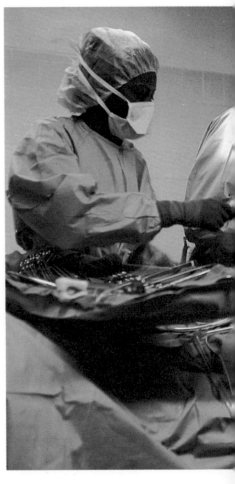

Why do we use alloys so much? The reason is that most metals by themselves do not have the right properties. Pure iron is quite a weak metal. But if you add a little carbon to it, it becomes much stronger. In fact most alloys are harder and stronger than the pure metals they are made from.

Metals are also added to one another to improve various other properties. One drawback with iron, for example, is that it corrodes, or rusts in damp air. But if you add nickel and chromium to iron, the alloy formed does not rust. This "stainless" steel now has all kinds of uses, from cutlery and car-body trim to surgeon's scalpels and chemical plants.

Steelmaking

The making of steel, our main alloy, is a great industry. It is made by refining, or purifying the pig iron that comes from the blast furnace. By itself, pig iron is not pure enough to be a useful metal. In particular, it contains too much carbon, from the coke

▷ *The jacket, or tower of the Magnus oil rig, ready for shipping out to the North Sea oil fields. The Magnus jacket is one of the biggest steel structures ever built. It is made up of eight miles of steel piping welded together. It measures nearly 975 feet high and weighs over 15,000 tons.*

▽ *Surgeons use stainless steel implements when they operate on patients. This steel alloy is ideal for the purpose because it does not affect the patient's body and is easy to clean. It contains nickel and chromium as well as iron.*

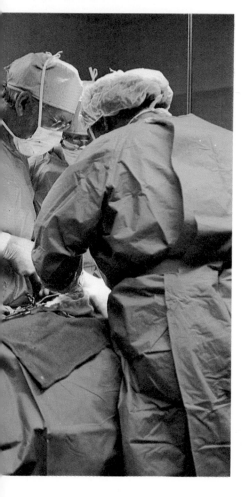

used for smelting in the blast furnace. The object of steelmaking is to burn out this carbon and remove many of the other impurities as well.

The most common method of steelmaking today is the basic-oxygen process. In this method a jet of oxygen is blasted into liquid pig iron. The carbon burns out in a spectacular fireworks display. Other impurities form a slag, which can then be separated from the refined steel. Some of the best steel is made in an electric furnace.

Clay and glass

From the beginnings of human history people have shown great ingenuity in using the materials around them to their advantage, starting with stone, wood, antlers, fish bones and even dirt and clay. Baked clay pots for cooking and storage were some of the first articles manufactured. And, despite the many new materials discovered or invented since, clay is still an invaluable manufacturing material. We use it to make pottery, bricks and tiles. Like our early ancestors, we make these products by shaping pieces of moist clay and then baking them in very hot ovens, or kilns. The clay sets hard and becomes strong.

Today we make a variety of other products by baking common earthy materials in kilns. By heating chalk and other rock, we can make cement, the main ingredient in concrete. By heating rocky materials such as alumina, we can make heat-resistant products, which we call refractories.

Pottery, bricks, tiles, and cement and refractories are all examples of what we call ceramics.

Pottery

Most of the pottery we use every day such as ordinary cups,

△ China clay is mined from pits in the ground, as here at Bodmin in Cornwall, England. The waste material is dumped into mountainous heaps. Brilliant white china clay is the purest clay used for making pottery. It is a powdery mixture of several minerals.

◁ These exquisite porcelain figures were made in Meissen, Germany, in 1770. Meissen was the first place in Europe to make porcelain, in about 1710. Before then only the Chinese knew the secret of making porcelain.

saucers and plates, is earthenware. This is a pottery made from rather cheap clay, which is baked, or "fired" at quite a low temperature (about 1800°F). As it comes out of the kiln, the pottery is dull and porous — it lets water through. So, to make it watertight, it has to be glazed, or given a glassy coating.

To make pottery that is watertight without glazing, different clays are required, and they must be fired at a higher temperature (up to 2500°F). One kind of watertight pottery is stoneware, which is used for such things as sewer pipes. The other kind is porcelain, which is used to make the finest pieces of pottery, and also electrical insulators.

One of the main ingredients in porcelain is china clay, or kaolin, which is the purest white. When the ingredients are fired, they melt together to form a kind of white glass. This is porcelain. Like glass, porcelain is translucent, or lets light through. And, of course, it is watertight. It therefore does not need to be glazed.

Pottery may be shaped in a variety of ways. The most common is "throwing," which means shaping a lump of wet clay while it is spinning on a wheel. Craft potters use their hands to do the shaping. In industry potters use simple machines called jiggers and jolleys for shaping.

▷ A potter shaping wet clay on a potter's wheel. This process is called throwing. The potter first places a lump of clay in the center of the wheel, and spins the wheel. She then skillfully uses her fingers to draw up the clay to form the walls and neck of the pot while the wheel is turning. After shaping, the pot is allowed to dry before it is fired in a kiln. It may then be decorated and glazed. Using a wheel, the potter can easily make circular shapes like cups, vases and jugs. She adds such things as the handle or lip of a jug later.

Glass

Glass is another common product made from one of the commonest materials around — sand. Ordinary window glass is known as soda lime glass because its ingredients include soda ash and lime. To make glass, very pure sand, soda ash and lime are heated in a furnace to about 3000°F. The mixture fuses, or melts together to form a red-hot liquid. When this liquid cools, it forms transparent glass.

Many glass objects, such as wine glasses and jars, are made by blowing. Air is blown into a blob of liquid, or molten, glass either by a human glassblower or by machine. The best sheet glass used for windows is made by floating a thin layer of glass on a bath of molten tin. The float glass produced is perfectly flat and has a natural sparkle. One interesting method of producing glass is in the form of fine fibers. Molten glass is forced through tiny holes either to form long threads or a glass "wool." Fiberglass threads are now widely used to reinforce, or strengthen plastics.

Experiment!

Roll out a lump of wet clay into a long "sausage." Also cut out a round disk for the bottom of the pot from a piece of flat clay.

Coil the long "sausage" of clay around the edge of the disk and then on top of itself. In this way you can build up the walls of the pot.

△ *Heat-resistant ceramic tiles cover the outside of the Space Shuttle. The tiles act as a heat shield to protect the astronauts inside when the shuttle re-enters the atmosphere after a mission. At this time friction (rubbing) of the air against the Shuttle produces high temperatures (up to 2700°F). The tiles are good insulators and stop the heat from getting through.*

When you have made the pot tall enough, smooth out the coils with your fingers inside and out. If you want to, you can then add some handles.

Tree products

The wood from trees has been one of our most useful materials from the dawn of civilization. Throughout the ages people have used wood to build houses, bridges, ships and boats and made it into weapons, machinery, furniture, and works of art. In the modern age we still use wood on a vast scale for building and making furniture. For this purpose it is unbeatable. It is relatively cheap, strong and tough, light, long-lasting and easy to work with. It also looks attractive.

Softwoods and hardwoods

Our wood comes from trees grown in natural or planted forests. Great natural forests grow in a large belt stretching across the cold lands of northern Europe, Asia and North America. They are forests of evergreen, or conifer trees, which are so called because they keep their leaves all year and bear their seeds in cones. They have sharp, needle-like leaves. In general their wood is relatively soft, and they are called softwoods. They include firs, spruces, cedars and pines. Most of the world's timber, the name for cut trees, comes from these softwood forests.

▽ The hulls of these sail boats are made from wood. Wood is the traditional material for boat-building. Boat-builders often build the hulls from plywood. This is a very strong material made by glueing together a number of plies, or thin sheets of wood. They are glued so that the grain (fiber direction) of each ply is at a right-angle to the grain on the plies on either side. This makes plywood much stronger than a piece of ordinary wood of the same size.

Birch   **Eucalyptus**   **Poplar**

Chain saw

Undercut

Spruce   **Pine**   **Fir**

◁ *We get our timber from a wide variety of trees. Many of these trees are grown specially in planted forests, or plantations. Foresters look after them throughout their life, and protect them from pests, diseases, and fire. It is a long job, because trees may take over a hundred years to grow big enough to be useful. The picture shows a few kinds of trees widely grown for their timber. Spruces, firs and pines are evergreen trees, which keep their leaves all year. They grow faster then most other trees.*

Forests of trees such as oak, beech, birch, elm, poplar and maple grow in warmer, moister climates farther south. They are broad-leaf trees, and are deciduous, which means they drop their leaves in autumn. Their wood is in general harder than that of the softwoods, and they are called hardwoods.

Felling and sawing

When the trees in the forest are big enough for cutting down, or felling, teams of lumberjacks move in. These days they use powerful chain saws to slice through the trunks. Before the lumberjack slices through the trunk, he makes a wedge-shaped undercut in the direction he wants the tree to fall. This makes the tree overbalance in this direction when it is cut.

The felled timber goes to the sawmills. In the sawmill it is sliced into planks by power saws. The timber cannot yet be used, however, because it is still green — it contains too much moisture. It is therefore stacked in the air to dry,

or is heated gently in kilns. This drying process is called seasoning. Seasoned wood is stronger and does not warp so much.

Pulping and processing

Large amounts of logs are turned into pulp for making paper (see opposite). This woodpulp is also the starting point of some man-made fibers. By treating the woodpulp with chemicals, it can be changed into raw materials for making rayon and acetate fibers. It can also be made into plastics, such as cellulose acetate, which is used to make photographic film. Cellulose is the main chemical compound in wood.

Other useful products can be obtained from the sap of certain trees. Most useful is rubber, which is made from the latex, or milky sap from rubber trees. The latex turns into solid "crude" rubber when it is treated with acid. Later, other materials, such as sulphur, are added to improve the rubber. With sulphur added, the rubber can be made stronger, harder and more elastic by heating.

Papermaking

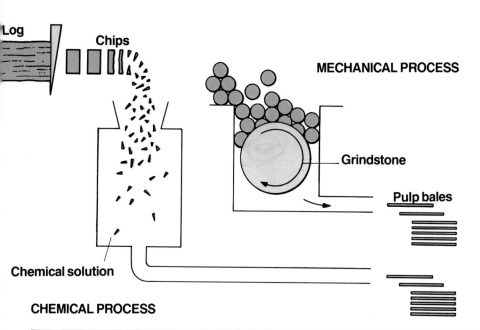

Log **Chips**

MECHANICAL PROCESS

Grindstone

Pulp bales

Chemical solution

CHEMICAL PROCESS

1 Paper is made from woodpulp. Woodpulp is produced from chopped-up logs at the pulpmill. In one pulping process, the logs are ground into fine fibers by a revolving grindstone. Water is sprayed on to keep the wood from overheating and charring. In another process, wood chips are cooked with a chemical solution. This breaks down the wood into fibers. The mass of fibers from either process is then dried and pressed into pulp paper.

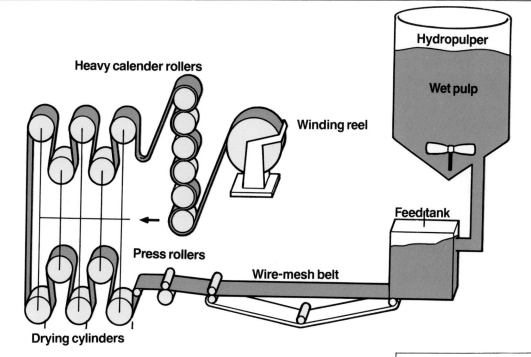

Heavy calender rollers

Winding reel

Hydropulper

Wet pulp

Feed tank

Press rollers

Wire-mesh belt

Drying cylinders

2 At the papermill the sheets of woodpulp are mixed with water to form a liquid rather like porridge. The liquid pulp is then poured into a moving wire-mesh belt. The water drains away, leaving a damp "blanket" of fibers. The blanket then goes through a series of heavy press rollers, which squeeze it into a thin sheet. The damp paper sheet next passes around a large number of heated cylinders, to dry it. Another set of heavy rollers gives it a smooth surface, and finally it is wound onto a reel at high speed.

Facts!
A forest the size of Wales must be cut down every year to supply enough paper for Britain. A forest the size of Sweden must be cut down every year to supply enough paper for the whole world.

Fibers

Life became a great deal warmer and more comfortable when people learned how to make textiles, or cloth, for clothing. Before, they had to wear animal skins. They first made cloth about 10,000 years ago, when they discovered how to spin and weave wool.

Wool is made up of fine curly fibers, which by themselves are quite short. But they can be twisted together and then drawn out into a long thread, or yarn. This is the process called spinning. For thousands of years, spinning was done by hand. About 500 years ago the spinning wheel came into use which speeded up the process. Then in the 1700s spinning machines such as the spinning jenny were invented. Today spinning machines work at an amazing rate. Some can produce over 300 feet of yarn a minute.

Weaving yarn into cloth is done on a loom. This is a machine for passing a length of yarn (the weft) back and forth under and over another set of yarns (the warp) stretched on a frame. You can see the kind of criss-cross pattern made by weaving in a handkerchief, which is typical woven product.

Natural fibers

Wool is one of many natural fibers that have been used for thousands of years. Today the best wool comes from the Australian Merino sheep. Another ancient fiber is cotton, which is obtained from the seed boll (pod) of the cotton plant. It grows in hot climates, such as the states in the southern part of the United States.

Flax has been grown for fiber for thousands of years. The fibers are found in the stem of the plant. Flax fibers are made into linen.

△ A silkworm spinning its cocoon of delicate silk fiber. When the cocoon is complete, it will contain more than a half mile of continuous thread. This comes from a spinning gland, or spinneret, in the silk worm's head. The silkworm is actually the larva, or caterpillar of a huge moth.

▷ A family sorting through the cotton they have just picked in cottonfields near Ica in Peru. The cotton is picked as fluffy balls from the seed pods of the shrubby cotton plant. Cotton fibers are quite short—up to about 2 inches long. They have to be spun into yarn before they can be woven into fabric.

▷ A craftswoman weaving on a hand loom. On the loom one set of yarns (the "warp") runs lengthwise, from back to front. They are threaded through wires in a device called a harness. The harness moves up or down, creating a gap between alternate threads. The weaver then passes a shuttle containing another thread (the "weft") through the gap at right angles to the warp. This process is repeated, the shuttle passing from side to side through the warp, making a new line of weave each time.

◁ *A mountaineer climbing up a mountain on a rope. The rope is made from nylon, one of the oldest and best of the synthetic fibers. Nylon is excellent for making climbing rope because it is very strong and waterproof. It also "gives" a little under strain, which prevents it from snapping easily. The mountaineer is also wearing a waterproof nylon parka and pants.*

▽*Nylon fibers are made by a process called melt spinning. Nylon chips are first melted. Then the molten liquid is forced through the tiny holes of a device called a spinneret. The fine streams of liquid that emerge harden into fibers when they hit the air.*

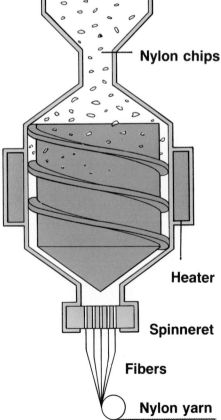

Nylon chips

Heater

Spinneret

Fibers

Nylon yarn

Artificial fibers

During the past hundred years or so the number of fibers for making textiles has grown enormously. And now most of our textiles are made of, or contain, one or more artificial, manufactured fibers. One of the oldest artificial fibers is rayon, also called viscose. It is made by treating woodpulp with chemicals. The fibers are actually thin threads of pure cellulose.

Other artificial fibers are made completely from chemicals. We call them synthetic fibers. Nylon (see above) was the first and is the best-known synthetic fiber. Other well-known synthetic fibers, often used for slacks, skirts and sweaters, include polyesters (such as Terylene and Dacron) and acrylics (such as Acrilan and Orlon).

Plastics

Over the past 30 years or so plastics have grown to be among our four most useful kinds of materials. The others are metals, concrete and wood. Today we write with plastic pens, drink from plastic cups, sit on plastic chairs, walk on plastic tiles, wear plastic shoes and coats, and wrap practically everything in plastic bags!

As you will have seen, there are many different kinds of plastics — some soft, some hard; some transparent, some colored; some flexible, some rigid. But although they are made of different materials, all plastics have two things in common. One, they

▽ *A pole vaulter springs into the air with his pole bent at an incredible angle. Any ordinary material would snap under the strain. But the pole is made from plastic strengthened with glass fibers. This material is often just called fiberglass.*

▷ *Plastics are made up of large molecules, with their atoms joined together in long chains. These large molecules are created by making small molecules join together to form long chains. Ethylene molecules, for example, can be made to combine together into long chains to form the plastic polythene.*

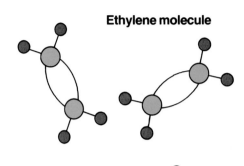

Ethylene molecule

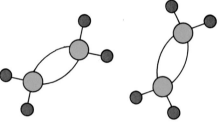

Polythene molecule

Carbon atoms

Hydrogen atoms

can be easily shaped by heating. Two, they are made up of long molecules in which the atoms are joined together in a long chain.

Polymerization

Most plastics are made from chemicals obtained from oil, or petroleum. They are made by a process called polymerization. Polymerization is a way of building up a lot of small molecules into the long-chain molecules typical of plastics. The smaller molecules are called monomers, and the long plastic molecules are called polymers. "Polymer" means "many parts." That is why the names of many plastics begin with "poly."

Many plastics are quite soft and fairly pliable and if you heat them, they start to melt. Polythene and nylon are like this. They are a kind of plastic known as a thermoplastic. Other plastics

△ Polythene film being made. In this machine molten polythene is squeezed out of a narrow circular slit. It cools and hardens into a thin transparent film. Air is blown through the middle of this tube of film. This way of shaping plastics is called extrusion.

◁ Bacon and eggs frying in a non-stick pan. The pan has been given a plastic coating to which nothing will stick. The plastic is known as PTFE, which is short for polytetrafluorethylene. It is a waxy substance rather like polythene, but is tougher and resistant to heat. It can be cleaned with a damp cloth.

are hard and rigid. The plastics used for light fittings, ash trays, and heat-proof surfaces are like this. They are called thermo-setting plastics. The plastics set rigid when they are first heat-shaped. No amount of reheating will cause them to melt again.

Better than nature

When plastics first came out, people often used to think they were cheap and nasty substitutes for natural materials. This certainly isn't true today. Modern plastics are excellent materials in their own right. They are often much better than natural materials for many uses.

Some plastics have properties no natural materials have. Nylon is used to make bearings, for example, in egg-beaters and food-mixers. These bearings need no oiling because nylon parts slide over one another easily.

▽This picture shows some of the many different plastics found in the kitchen at home. One of the commonest is PVC, short for polyvinyl chloride. Washable wallpaper, aprons and vinyl flooring are made from PVC and similar plastics. Many items are molded — the plastics are forced into a shaped mold. This is the commonest method of shaping plastics.

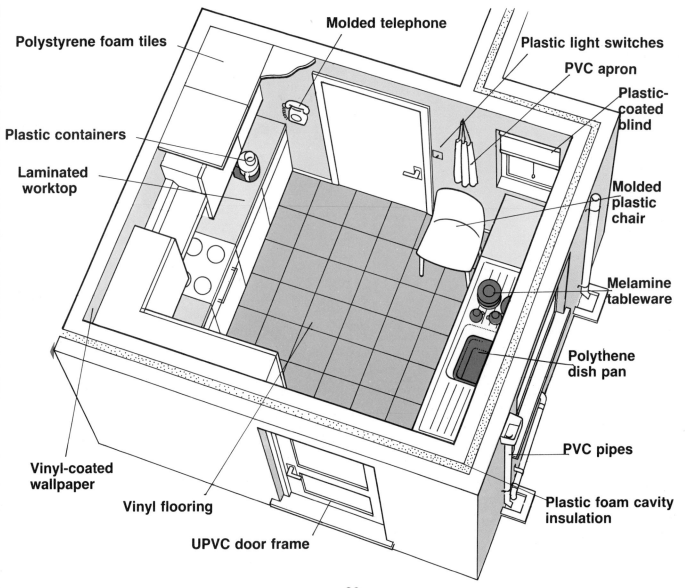

Polystyrene foam tiles

Molded telephone

Plastic light switches

PVC apron

Plastic-coated blind

Plastic containers

Laminated worktop

Molded plastic chair

Melamine tableware

Polythene dish pan

PVC pipes

Vinyl-coated wallpaper

Vinyl flooring

UPVC door frame

Plastic foam cavity insulation

Shaping materials

Some kinds of materials are easy to shape. We can shape wood by whittling with a knife, cutting with a saw, smoothing with a plane, or boring holes with a drill. Because wood is a soft material you can use simple hand tools to shape it.

Shaping metal is not easy because it is a very much harder and tougher material. To saw, cut, plane or drill metal, you have to use power tools. In industry engineers use powered shaping machines called machine tools. On these machines the workpiece, or piece of metal to be shaped, is clamped in position and then cut. This process is called machining.

The most common machining operation is turning, which takes place on a lathe (see picture, right). Another is milling. In milling, metal is cut from the workpiece by a spinning toothed cutting wheel. In drilling, rotating drill bits are lowered onto the workpiece. Most drill presses, as the machines are called, can hold several sized drills at once, and can drill different-sized holes in quick succession.

◁ Molten steel is poured into molds at a steelworks at Duna in Hungary. When it cools, the metal will set solidly and take the shape of the mold. This casting process produces blocks called ingots, which are then shaped further by forging or rolling.

Hot metal

Most metal parts are machined to their final size and shape after they have been roughly shaped first. Some parts are cast into shape. Molten metal is poured into a mold of the required shape, and allowed to set just like jello sets in a mold. Casting is a process also used for shaping many other materials as well, including glass, plastics and clay.

Often casting is used as a preliminary shaping process for metal to produce simple blocks called ingots, which then go for further shaping. One simple process for shaping ingots is rolling. A red-hot ingot passes through sets of heavy rollers, which squeeze it thinner and thinner and make it longer.

Ingots may also be hammered into shape by a falling hammer on a machine called a drop forge. This machine does the same job as the blacksmith. Other machines shape the metal, not with sharp hammer blows, but with a gradual squeezing action. They are known as hydraulic presses.

△ A huge turbine shaft being shaped on a giant lathe. The shaft is "turned," or rotated, and then sharp cutting tools are moved into it to cut away metal until it is the correct size and shape. Here an engineer is checking the diameter with a special gauge.

△ A traveling blacksmith at work. He is practicing one of the oldest methods of shaping metal — hammer forging. He heats up a piece of iron in a hot fire until it becomes red-hot and pliable. Then he hammers it into shape on an anvil.

◁ Molding a boat hull in fiberglass, which is properly called GRP (glass-reinforced plastic). The hull is made by spraying a mixture of glass fibers and plastics onto a steel mold of the required shape. It is built up layer by layer. When the plastic sets hard, it takes the shape of the mold. GRP is now sometimes even used to build small ships.

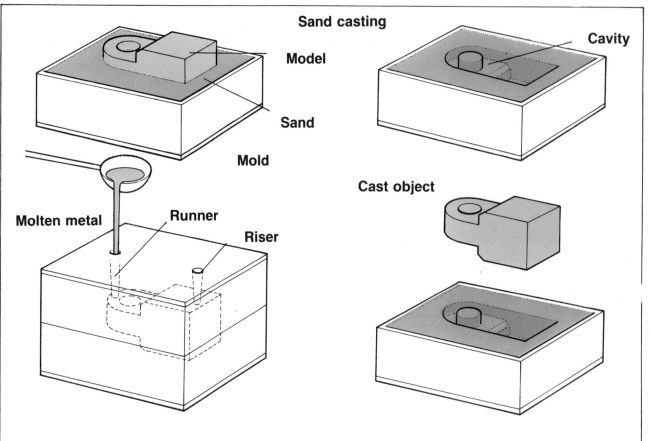

Sand casting

Model

Sand

Mold

Molten metal

Runner

Riser

Cavity

Cast object

Many metal parts are shaped by casting. Molten metal is poured into a hollow mold of the required shape. When the metal cools, it sets in the shape of the mold. Sand molds are often used. First, a mixture of sand and clay is packed around a model of the object required. Then the model is removed. This is done separately for the top and bottom halves. Then the two halves are put together. This leaves a hollow cavity inside. Molten metal is then poured in through a channel ("runner") to the cavity. Another channel ("riser") allows the air inside to escape. When the cavity is full, the metal is left to cool. The mold is then broken apart, and the cast object removed.

Joining materials

On this and the following pages some of the most common methods of joining materials are illustrated and described. They are each useful for certain purposes and materials. Wood can simply be joined by careful cutting so that the pieces push-fit together. The wood "gives" slightly as the pieces are pushed home so they fit tightly. Metal cannot be joined in this way because it does not "give" enough to form a tight joint.

To join metal you need something much stronger. Nuts and bolts are useful for joining pieces that may need to be taken apart. But sometimes the nuts can unscrew by themselves, loosening or breaking the joint. Riveting gives a more secure joint, but you cannot take it apart. The strongest joint of all is made by welding. Parts of the metal pieces to be joined are actually melted together so there is no real join at all, just continuous metal.

Nuts and bolts
Nuts and bolts are used to join together the hundreds of pieces of Meccano in this model of an offshore oil rig. Nuts and bolts are also widely used to join metal parts in many kinds of real machines too. Hundreds are used in an automobile, for example. Most nuts are hexagonal, or six-sided. They are tightened up with a wrench. Bolts may also have a hexagonal head, but some have a screw head and are tightened with a screwdriver.

▽*A close-up of a nut and bolt, showing the hexagonal head and nut, and the screw threads.*

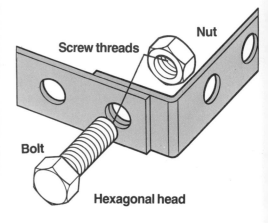

Screw threads · Nut

Bolt

Hexagonal head

Joinery

Carpenters may join pieces of wood together by carefully shaping the edges to be joined, and then fitting them tightly together. This picture shows a dove-tail joint between two pieces of wood at right-angles. Can you see why it is called a dove-tail?

Nails and screws

Carpenters also join pieces of wood together by hammering a nail through them. The head of the nail helps keep the top piece from pulling off. They can do a better job by screwing the pieces together. The threads of the screw keep it firmly in place.

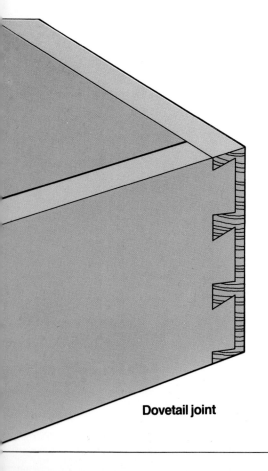

Dovetail joint

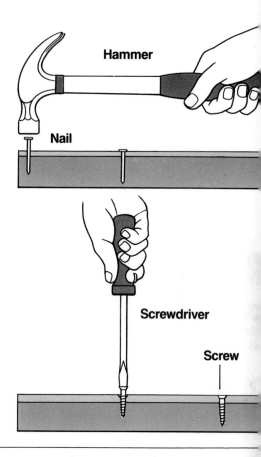

Hammer

Nail

Screwdriver

Screw

It also sticks handles to teapots. ARALDITE

Adhesives

This picture shows a real car stuck to a billboard by glue. No ordinary glues could do this. They are made from bones, gums and rubber solution, and are quite weak. The adhesive used here is made from plastic materials called epoxy resins and is incredibly strong. It comes in the form of two packs containing pasty substances which have to be mixed together before use. In a short time the adhesive hardens and bonds virtually any two materials together. Epoxy resins are now widely used for sticking metal parts together, in the aircraft industry, for example.

Rivets

The Queen Mary *is one of the biggest ocean liners ever built, measuring 1,019 feet long. She once used to travel across the Atlantic but now is moored at Long Beach in California and used as a hotel. Her hull is constructed of thousands of steel plates, which are joined together by no fewer than 10 million rivets.*

▽*A rivet is a kind of threadless bolt. It is pushed through the holes in two metal plates and hammered at the end to form another head. This locks it firmly in place.*

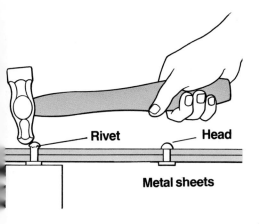

Rivet **Head**

Metal sheets

Welding

A welder at work with a gas torch. He uses the hot flame to soften the edges of the pieces of metal to be joined. Then he adds extra molten metal into the joint from a so-called filler rod in his right hand. When the metal cools, the two pieces of metal are firmly joined, or welded together. The torch is called an oxyacetylene torch because it burns oxygen and acetylene gases to make the hot flame.

Design and testing

In the modern world new products come onto the market every day, from detergents and dresses to cars and airliners. A great deal of thought and effort go into a product before it appears. The manufacturers often first carry out market research to see if people would buy such a product, if it were available. Then they set out to design it.

They have to consider many things when they start to design. First and foremost, the product must work — it must be functional. A plane must be able to fly, a gun to fire. The product must also be sold at the right price. If it is too expensive, people won't buy it. If it is too cheap, the manufacturers won't make any profit. In many cases, the product must also look nice, to attract customers.

Materials and shape

When building machines and structures, manufacturers must choose a suitable material. This must be strong enough to take the load, or weight, on it. It might also have to stand up to other things, such as chemicals or heat. Ordinary steel, for example, could not be used in a chemical plant making sulphuric acid because it would dissolve away. Stainless steel would, however, be suitable because it resists chemical attack.

Shape is important in the design of many machines and structures, because the shape often affects how their designs behave. The shape of aircraft, for example, is very important. A badly designed aircraft experiences too much air resistance, or drag.

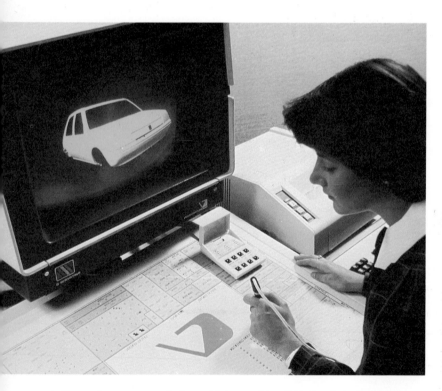

△ Computers are now being widely used in all kinds of design work. This is known as computer-aided design (CAD). Here a designer is using the computer to help her improve a design for a family car. She feeds information into the computer about the kind of car she wants — how many people it should carry, how many doors, how fast it should go, and so on. The computer then comes up with a suitable design. The designer may then make a model of the design and test it in a wind tunnel.

◁ An engineer is preparing a model of an offshore oil rig for testing in a wind tunnel. Note that it is mounted upside down. In the wind-tunnel test, air is blown past the model at various speeds. Engineers then observe what effect this has on the model. Such tests give them a good idea of how a full-size oil rig would behave in real life at sea particularly in stormy weather.

◁ A Concorde supersonic airliner undergoing a vibration test. Machines are attached to the body and vibrate it for days, even months at a time. Vibration testing is important because metal parts weaken much more easily when they are vibrated. They weaken because of what is called metal fatigue. Metal fatigue caused a number of the first jet airliners, the Comets, to crash. The dangerous effects of metal fatigue can be reduced by careful design and construction.

This wastes fuel and can be dangerous. A well-designed aircraft is smooth and streamlined so that its body "slips" easily through the air.

One flying machine in which the shape did not have to be smooth and streamlined was the lunar landing module flown by Apollo astronauts down to the Moon. This was an odd-looking, flimsy contraption with bits and pieces sticking out everywhere. This did not matter because it was designed to fly in space, not in air. It could be built flimsily because of the Moon's low gravity, which means the materials would have to support low weight.

Testing, testing

Testing plays a great part in the production of a product. New planes and cars, for example, are tested thoroughly during the design and production stages. These tests are carried out on individual parts and on the complete machines. A car's suspension system, for example, is tested by apparatus that imitates the pounding of a car wheel over a bumpy road. Instruments check how well the springs and shock absorbers of the system behave. After the tests, the system may have to be changed.

Testing is particularly important with aircraft, because the lives of perhaps hundreds of people depend on the craft being perfectly safe. Every part is tested thoroughly, often to destruction.

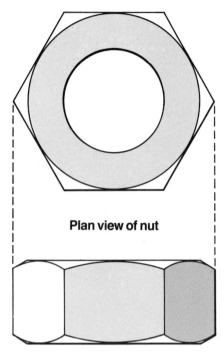

Plan view of nut

Elevation

△ A simple example of an engineering drawing, of an ordinary nut. Such a drawing shows how the nut looks from different viewpoints. Detailed engineering drawings are always made of every part when the design is complete. From these drawings engineers can then manufacture the parts.

◁ Many manufacturers test their new designs to destruction. Car manufacturers, for example, deliberately crash their cars to see what effects the crash will have on the car and passengers inside it. Instead of real passengers, they put dummies in the seats. The dummies are wired up with probes that tell the test engineers what "injuries" they suffer in the crash.

Materials for cars

How many different parts do you think an ordinary family car has — 50, 100, 1,000? In fact it has as many as 10,000 individual parts! They vary from tiny screws and nuts and bolts to the all-in-one body shell and massive engine block. The car is by far the most complicated machine we normally come across. Yet it is so carefully designed and is made of such carefully chosen materials that in general it is capable of providing many years of reliable transportation, totalling perhaps 100,000 miles.

As many as 50 different kinds of materials are used to make the various parts of a car. They are carefully selected according to what the part has to do. The most common material is steel. This is used for the body shell and for other parts of the structure. Steel is strong but it has the great disadvantage that it corrodes, or rusts away. For protection, the body is coated on the outside with paint, which also decorates, and underneath with a bitumen "undercoating." Nevertheless, rusting always begins after a few years. To beat the rusting problem, a few cars have bodies made of fiberglass.

The other great mass of metal is in the engine block, which is usually made of cast iron. Some cars, however, have aluminum blocks. Other metals include copper, which is used for the wiring that circulates electricity to various parts of the car. Some of the many other materials used in car manufacture are shown on the next page.

▽*A Formula One racing car pictured at speed during a Grand Prix. The lightest possible materials, such as aluminum and fiberglass are used in its construction. The lighter it is, the faster it can go for the same engine power. Racing cars go so fast that they tend to lift off the ground and start to "fly" at times. To stop this from happening, they are fitted with airfoils, a kind of upside-down wing, at the front and back. When the airfoils travel through the air, the air pressure pushes them downward, and this helps the car stick to the track.*

Paintwork
This is needed to protect and decorate the steel body. Paint is applied by spray and dries to form a thin plastic coating.

Gasoline
This is the substance burned in the engine to provide power. It is a product made from petroleum and it vaporizes easily.

Tires
These are designed with a tread that keeps the car firmly on the road and helps prevent skidding in wetness. They also help cushion the ride for passengers. They are made from synthetic rubber, a kind of elastic plastic.

Bodywork
This consists of shaped sheets of steel, welded together into a stiff structure, or shell.

Coil springs
These form part of the car's suspension system. They coil and uncoil as the car goes over bumps, making the ride more comfortable. They are made from special alloy steel which allows them to be flexible but strong.

Undercoating
This is applied underneath the body to keep water off the metal and prevent rusting. It is a kind of tarry material.

Battery
This provides the electricity for the car, to run lights, windshield wipers, horn, and so on. It contains lead plates in a solution of sulphuric acid.

Brake linings
These are pressed against the wheel discs or drums to slow down the car when the brakes are applied. They are made of tough heat-resistant materials, such as asbestos.

Grease
Some bearings are lubricated with grease. This is a thick substance obtained from petroleum and sometimes has graphite (a form of carbon) added.

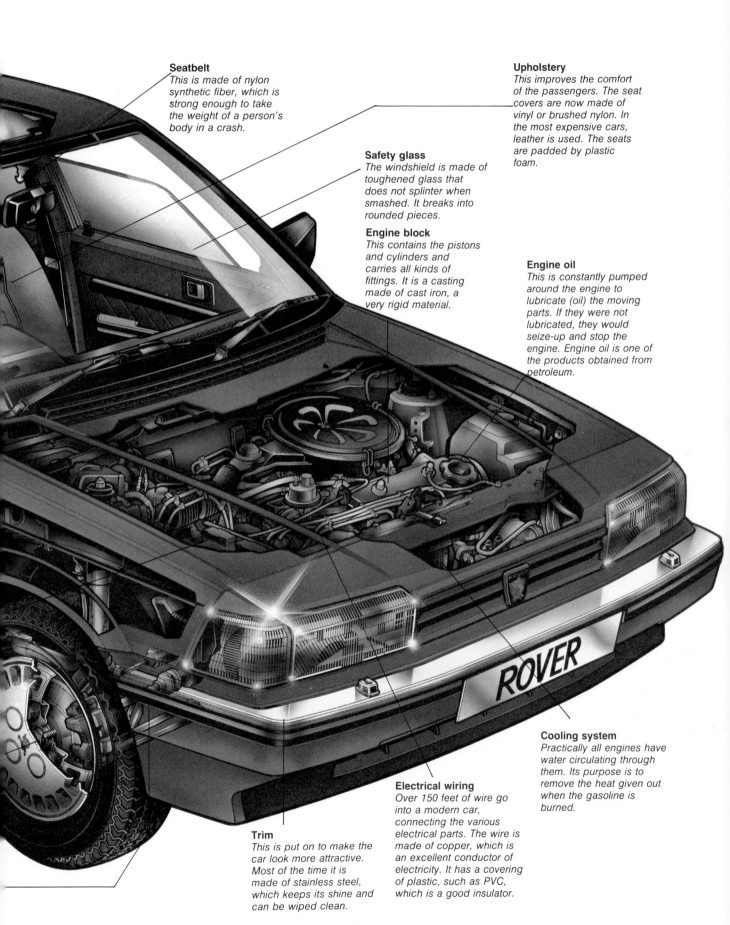

Seatbelt
This is made of nylon synthetic fiber, which is strong enough to take the weight of a person's body in a crash.

Safety glass
The windshield is made of toughened glass that does not splinter when smashed. It breaks into rounded pieces.

Engine block
This contains the pistons and cylinders and carries all kinds of fittings. It is a casting made of cast iron, a very rigid material.

Upholstery
This improves the comfort of the passengers. The seat covers are now made of vinyl or brushed nylon. In the most expensive cars, leather is used. The seats are padded by plastic foam.

Engine oil
This is constantly pumped around the engine to lubricate (oil) the moving parts. If they were not lubricated, they would seize-up and stop the engine. Engine oil is one of the products obtained from petroleum.

Cooling system
Practically all engines have water circulating through them. Its purpose is to remove the heat given out when the gasoline is burned.

Electrical wiring
Over 150 feet of wire go into a modern car, connecting the various electrical parts. The wire is made of copper, which is an excellent conductor of electricity. It has a covering of plastic, such as PVC, which is a good insulator.

Trim
This is put on to make the car look more attractive. Most of the time it is made of stainless steel, which keeps its shine and can be wiped clean.

51

Buildings around the world

In most large cities of the world the new buildings going up look much alike. Because land is scarce in the cities, builders build upward, creating aptly named "skyscrapers." Skyscrapers are constructed mainly of concrete and glass, and few have any real character. The ordinary houses in suburban areas also tend to look alike. They are often built of bricks and mortar with shingled roofs.

Local materials

The really interesting dwellings are usually found in rural and undeveloped areas, where traditional methods of building still go on. The houses are built with local materials that come easily to hand. In the frozen north, Eskimos sometimes build igloos, which are circular huts made using blocks of frozen snow. In many hot climates, such as Mexico and Egypt, the people build houses of mud bricks, or adobe. Some adobe houses are quite large, as you can see in the picture. But in many countries mud dwellings are much smaller and simpler. They are usually boxlike and have flat roofs and tiny windows, which help keep out the heat of the sun. They are often painted white to reflect the Sun's heat.

For obvious reasons mud houses are of no use in regions with heavy rainfall, such as in the rain forests of the tropics. There, because of the heat, flimsier materials may be used. The houses

▷These tent-like dwellings can be found in the Mongolian desert. They are called yurts. They are the homes of a nomadic people. Yurts are usually circular in shape and are built with a frame of wooden poles. The frame is covered with skins or textiles, which are often woven in bright colors. Inside their yurts, the nomads make themselves comfortable with thick, brightly colored rugs.

△The huts in this village near Lake Turkana, in northern Kenya, are made from branches and palm fronds. They were built by the Turkana tribe, who lead a mainly nomadic life. They are always on the move, and so they build their dwellings of handy local materials, obtained from thorn bushes and palm trees.

△ Adobe houses on the Tewa Indian Reservation in New Mexico. They are built from bricks made of mud and straw. These materials are

mixed together and shaped into bricks, which are then laid out to dry in the sun. When dry, the bricks are laid using a mud mortar to bond them.

are constructed mainly of wooden planks and poles and are roofed with overlapping palm fronds. They are often built on stilts above the rivers to protect the inhabitants from dangerous insects and wild animals, and also from flooding. The rivers also make safer and more reliable highways than jungle tracks.

Some of the jungle dwellings are particularly interesting. The appropriately named longhouses of Borneo, for example, are made large enough to house the whole village! They are built by the Dyak people and can be up to 115 feet long and 65 feet wide. They can house as many as 50 families.

More solid wood construction is carried out in cooler climates farther north in regions that are heavily wooded. Wood is a good insulator and helps keep out the winter cold. Timber houses are particularly favored in Scandinavia and North America.

On the move

People in many parts of the world lead a nomadic life, moving from place to place to find new pastures for their livestock. This happens especially in desert regions where grazing is sparse. These people can have no permanent homes. They either build makeshift shelters of local materials, or live in tents they carry around with them.

◁ These stilt houses, on the Sepic River in Papua New Guinea, are made from timber cut locally in the jungle. This type of house is often built in jungle regions with heavy rainfall.

▽High-rise apartment and office buildings are mushrooming in Hong Kong because land is scarce there. Like skyscrapers all over the world, they are made from steel and concrete.

Construction site

Among the biggest users of materials are the people we call civil engineers. These are the engineers who build bridges, dams, skyscrapers, roads, tunnels and pipelines. These structures use unbelievable amounts of materials. The cables that support the Verrazano-Narrows suspension bridge in New York contain enough steel wire to stretch five times around the world.

Concrete and steel are the civil engineers' main construction materials, which enable them to build vast structures. The two are often used together in the form of reinforced concrete. This is made by pouring concrete onto a framework of steel rods. The steel rods greatly strengthen the concrete. In particular they prevent the concrete from sagging.

Earth movers

In any construction project the first step is to prepare the site. This usually means clearing away any existing buildings or natural obstacles such as trees and rocks. Often, large amounts of dirt, or earth have to be moved to level the site or prepare it for the next stage of construction — laying the foundation. In site clearance you see a variety of powerful machines in action, including bulldozers and excavators.

Bulldozers are powerful tractors with crawler, or caterpillar tracks, which enable them to travel easily over rough ground. They have a tough curved blade in front to knock things down or push them out of the way. Excavators are digging machines.

▷ Clearing a construction site in the middle of a town. One building has been knocked down, and a much higher one will be built to take full advantage of the limited space available. Two excavators are shown here. They each have a long arm, which is moved hydraulically, or by means of liquid pressure, but with different attachments on the ends of the arms. The one in front has a pneumatic drill to break up the concrete. The other has a digging bucket for removing soil and rubble. The excavators have caterpillar, or crawler tracks so that they can move easily over rough ground.

◁ A skyscraper under construction in San Francisco. It is built with a rigid frame of steel girders. This will carry all the weight of the building. The walls will carry no weight at all, and can be made of flimsy materials, such as aluminum.

RAFT FOUNDATIONS

Reinforced concrete slab

Two kinds of foundations are used to support skyscrapers. Tall buildings must have strong foundations, otherwise they will sink into the ground under their own weight and probably collapse. If the soil at the building site is firm, then a skyscraper can be built with a raft foundation.

Firm foundations

Whatever structure is to be built, it must have a firm base, or foundation, to support all its weight under all conditions. The best foundations are solid rock, which cannot "give." Some of the tallest buildings in the world are found in Manhattan, because solid rock lies close to the surface there. The tallest building there at present is the World Trade Center, which towers to 1,350 feet. Elsewhere, rock usually lies too far down to be reached. Then raft or pile foundations of reinforced concrete have to be used (see right). The type of foundation chosen depends on the strength of the soil.

For bridges, foundations often need to be built underwater.

PILE FOUNDATIONS

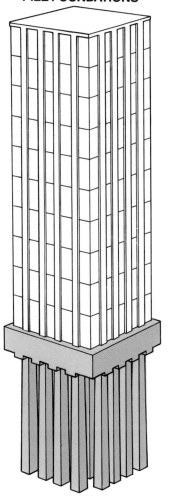

Reinforced concrete piles

This is simply a large slab of reinforced concrete. If the soil is soft and weak, the skyscraper must be built on concrete piles driven deep into the ground.

They are sometimes built from caissons. These are ready-built concrete structures that are sunk into position on the river bed and filled with concrete.

Superstructure

The part of a structure above the ground is called the superstructure. In most civil engineering projects the superstructure is built of steel or concrete or both. It is the great strength of steel that enables huge structures to be built, like the 1,454 foot tall Sears Tower in Chicago, the world's tallest building. The steel frames of skyscrapers carry all the weight of the buildings. In ordinary buildings, however, the walls carry all the weight.

Bridges

Bridges are among the most spectacular structures built by civil engineers. Take, for example, the Humber Bridge in north-east England, which has the largest span (distance between supports) in the world. It spans a width of no less than 4,626 feet. Its twin towers are 530 feet tall. They are so far apart that they have to be built slightly out of parallel to allow for the curvature of the Earth!

The Humber Bridge is an example of a suspension bridge. The bridge deck, which carries the traffic, hangs (is suspended) from a pair of thick cables, made of high-strength steel wires. The suspension bridge is a modern version of the rope bridge used by people throughout the world for thousands of years.

Arch bridges are also widely used and can

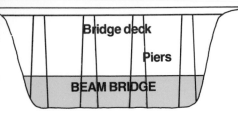

The Sydney Harbor Bridge in Sydney, New South Wales, Australia. It is perhaps the finest steel-arch bridge in the world, with a span of nearly 1,650 feet.

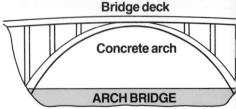

A beam bridge is the simplest type of bridge. To span a wide gap it must have many supporting piers. Otherwise it would collapse in the middle.

This arch bridge is made of concrete. The bridge deck is carried on the top of the arch. In steel-arch bridges, the deck often runs through the arch.

comfortably span gaps of up to about 1625 feet. They may be built of reinforced concrete or steel. The strength of the bridge lies in the shape of the arch, which carries the weight down to the ground.

The simplest bridges are beam bridges. They have a deck of girders or reinforced concrete, with piers underneath to support it. The piers have to be quite close together, otherwise the deck will sag in the middle. Using the cantilever principle, it is possible to span wider gaps. A cantilever is a beam that is anchored at one end and supported in the middle. The other end overhangs. So when you put two cantilevers together, the double overhang becomes quite a long span.

△ *The Golden Gate suspension bridge in San Francisco, California.*

▽ *The deck of a suspension bridge hangs from thick steel cables, which go up and over tall suspension towers. The cables are firmly anchored at each end.*

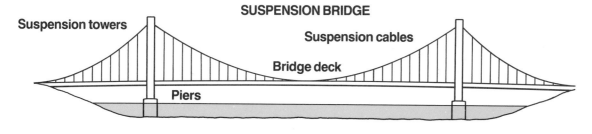

SUSPENSION BRIDGE

Suspension towers

Suspension cables

Bridge deck

Piers

Dams

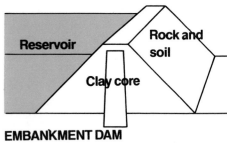

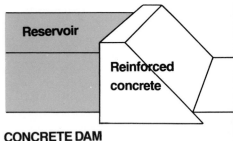

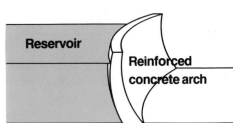

△ The three main types of dam. Embankment dams are built mainly with rock and soil. Concrete and arch dams are constructed of reinforced concrete.

◁ The Itaipu Dam under construction in South America.

Dams are the most massive of all human-made structures. The biggest are constructed of hundreds of millions of cubic feet of rock and dirt. They are known as earth-fill, or embankment dams.

Concrete is the other main material for building dams. A typical concrete dam is triangular in cross-section. It stays in position because of its weight, and is an example of a gravity dam. Less concrete is needed to build an arch dam. This gets its strength from the shape of its arch (just as the arch bridge does).

Dams are built across rivers for many reasons. They are often built for water storage. The water builds up behind the dam to create an artificial lake, or reservoir. By increasing the water level navigation may also be improved. Often the water stored is used to drive the turbines which produce electricity in a hydroelectric power station.

Animal builders

Human beings are not the only creatures that can build impressive structures. In their own way some animals are far more expert at building than the most brilliant human architect. But their building sense is instinctive. They are urged to build by mysterious forces inside them. They build homes for many reasons — to escape from predators, to shelter from the weather, to store food and to raise their young.

The tunnelers

An enormous number of animals burrow into the ground to make their homes. Rabbits, hamsters, gophers, badgers and moles do this. The mole is the most expert tunneler and is well adapted for its life underground, with spade-like feet and sensitive snout and whiskers. It comes to the surface so rarely that its eyes are virtually useless. The burrows of many animals form a complicated network of tunnels, with chambers leading off for different purposes, such as food stores and nurseries.

▽ *Termites built this huge mound in the Luangwa Valley in Zambia. Some mounds reach more than 22 feet high. They grow when termites bring soil up to the surface as they tunnel in the ground in search of food.*

One of the more interesting burrowers is the trapdoor spider of Jamaica. It burrows into the ground and lines its burrow with silk thread and saliva. The spider makes a strong well-fitting lid to cover the entrance and attaches it by a silken hinge so that it can open and close easily.

The nesters

The most skilled nesting creatures, of course, are birds, or rather some birds. But they are not the only nest builders in the animal world. The harvest mouse constructs very fine nests up to 3 feet above the ground in tall grasses and reeds. First it binds the plant stems together with long strips of leaves it has shredded in its mouth.

Then it begins making a rounded nest with the same materials, finishing off with a domed roof.

Squirrels also build comfortable nests, which are called dreys. They build them of twigs and branches or perhaps patch up discarded birds' nests. A squirrel may build a number of nests in nearby trees for different purposes.

There is considerable variety among the nest building habits of the birds. Some, particularly the sea birds, virtually build no nest at all, often laying their eggs in simple hollows in the ground. Some build primitive nests. Wood pigeons make a simple platform of twigs on a branch. The majority of birds, though, build

◁ Woodpeckers build their homes by drilling holes in dead trees with their chisel-like beaks. This one is the hairy woodpecker from North America. Woodpeckers can be heard in most forests during the spring when they drill their nests and drum on hollow branches to warn off rivals.

▷ Weaver birds build beautiful nests of interwoven grasses. The entrance to the nest is at the bottom and may be a tunnel. This particular bird is a male masked weaver bird. He is hanging upside-down as part of his courtship display.

△ Beavers built this dam across a stream in Alaska. They make dams with great skill, using logs, branches, mud and stones. The dams are built to deepen water where they have built their lodge, or home. Beavers like the water to be deep enough to cover the entrance to the lodge.

well-made cup-shaped nests from twigs and grasses, usually woven into a living branch.

The weavers

Some of the smaller European birds weave rounded nests of moss, lichen, spiders' webs and down. But the most intricate weaving is done by the various species of weaver birds that live in tropical and semi-tropical parts of the world.

The male weaver bird builds the nest by weaving strips of grass through the branches and looping them to form a rounded shape. The bird completes the nest by carefully interweaving grasses

◁ Wild honeybees have built this nest. It is the home of perhaps tens of thousands of workers, a few drones (males) and a solitary queen. The workers carry out all the work in the hive. They make beeswax and use it to construct a network of six-sided compartments, or cells. This forms the honeycomb. You can see this construction clearly in the picture.

through the basic structure, often using knots to keep the strands in place. The sociable weaver birds of the African grasslands build nests jointly to make an impressive communal nest. It may grow year by year to a diameter of nearly 33 feet, and house perhaps 30 pairs of birds.

There are also so-called weaver ants, which make their nests by joining leaves together. They join them in an interesting way. They first pull the edges of two adjacent leaves together and then use their own larvae (young) as a kind of weaving shuttle. They squeeze the larvae, which give out a sticky silken thread, and they use this to bond the leaf edges together.

The engineers

Pride of place among the engineers of the animal world must be given to the beavers. They build the most effective structures to dam the streams in which they have their homes, or lodges (see pages 62/63). They may even alter the height of the dam to suit the rate of water flow. Considering the beavers' limited tools —

just teeth and paws — the dams are a remarkable achievement.

The civil engineers of the insect kingdom are the ant look-alikes we call termites, of which there are some 170 species. These are the creatures that build the gigantic mounds seen in the tropical regions of Africa, Australia and elsewhere (see page 61). The outside of a termite mound is usually coated with a substance made from termite "dung." It feels as hard as concrete and gives some protection against predators. One interesting species is the compass termites of Australia. They build their wedge-shaped mounds so that the short sides face north-south. This helps to keep the mound cool.

The most intricate structures in the insect world, though, are the wax honeycombs built by bees, which have a perfect hexagonal structure (see above). Some wasps, the social wasps, make a similar structure from cellulose. It is, in fact, a kind of paper that the wasps make by chewing wood and other plant material.

Index

1 2 3 4 5 6 7 8 9 10—WOR—95 94 93 92 91 90 89 88 87 86